NORTHBOUND LIGHTS

TRACKS ACROSS MICHIGAN AND WISCONSIN

D. C. JESSE BURKHARDT

AMERICA
THROUGH
TIME

Also by D. C. Jesse Burkhardt in the America Through Time series:
Traces of the Ann Arbor Railroad (ISBN: 978-1-63499-297-8)

Back cover photographs—clockwise, upper left to right: CSX freight yard in Ludington, Michigan; Soo Line signal tower at Ashland, Wisconsin; Canadian National southbound at Junction City, Wisconsin.

All photographs by D. C. Jesse Burkhardt, except where otherwise indicated.

America Through Time®
An imprint of Sutton Publishing Inc
www.through-time.com
office@through-time.com

First published 2023
Reprinted 2025

ISBN 978-1-63499-461-3

Typeset in Mrs Eaves XL Serif Narrow
Printed and bound in the United States of America

Contents

Acknowledgments

Many years of history went into the motivation for this book. Being born and raised in a Midwestern town with multiple rail lines will do that to you.

I want to express strong appreciation to Alan Sutton and Kena Smith of Fonthill Media of Stroud, England, for their belief in *Northbound Lights* and for its stellar execution.

For several wonderful photo submissions, thanks to Peter Hayes and Dennis Schmidt, two photographers whose work I admire.

For the state railroad maps, appreciation to the Michigan Department of Transportation and Wisconsin Department of Transportation.

Thanks to James Chapman of Gorge Ink in White Salmon, Washington, for superb technical assistance and photo scans, and Pro Photo Supply of Portland, Oregon, for sharp work scanning my slide film.

Thanks to Dean Sauvola and the "Railroads of the Lake Superior Region" Facebook site for info assists.

Thanks to the Cabbage Shed in Elberta, Michigan, for being a valued oasis over the decades.

On a personal level, I would like to note how much I value the friendships of several guys who shared the Jackson, Michigan, tracks with me when I was a young kid in grade school seeking adventure: Jim Stanaway, Tom Lacinski, and Scott Sparling all felt an enthusiasm for hanging out by the New York Central/Penn Central railroad tracks in our hometown. It was a special time and place to be boys and those are some sacred memories. In later years, thanks also to Larry "Moon" Yaek, for sharing railroad experiences across this region of the country, from heartland towns such as Cadillac and Cheboygan in Michigan to Ladysmith and Superior in Wisconsin.

Family ties: Love to Renae and Clare; to my brothers Ron and Chris for the memories of the "meetings at the crossroads" in our Kensington house; and to Dad and Mom for providing me with those Michigan roots and support spanning seven decades. It was my father's U.S. Army training stints at Fort McCoy in Wisconsin that helped further my interest in and appreciation for my "sister state" of Wisconsin.

In memoriam—to my uncle, Vaughn D. Ordway, who hired on with New York Central as a fireman in 1916; later served as a yard, road, and passenger service engineer; and retired in 1968 after decades of service with NYC in Jackson.

And of course, affection and thanks to all the railroads and crews that made these scenes possible.

INTRODUCTION

Growing up in Jackson, Michigan, in the early 1960s was a railroad paradise. I lived in the house my parents built at 1521 Kensington Drive—a peaceful and quiet house in a suburban neighborhood—for eighteen years before moving first to Ann Arbor and then to Ypsilanti. Ironically, those were the next two towns to the east along the New York Central mainline that passed through Jackson.

No fewer than eight rail routes radiated from my hometown, a central hub with eight spokes reaching in every direction. Seven of the lines were New York Central. The other one was Grand Trunk Western.

The active NYC east–west track near my boyhood home originated from a large freight yard in Jackson and sliced southwest from there to get to Elkhart, Indiana. It was a sleek, fast, modern mainline with signal towers every couple of miles and sidings that were activated remotely, allowing trains to pass each other without crews needing to stop and turn switches, thereby speeding the movement of goods.

There was something special about living near a busy New York Central mainline and having a few good friends who also felt a connection to the tracks and trains cutting through the fields near our neighborhood. The first time I got close to the tracks, I must have been in first or second grade. The infrastructure—twin steel rails heading off to the unseen horizon on a bed of gravel and wooden ties—sparked such a sense of mystery within me that I surreptitiously pocketed a couple rocks from the roadbed and kept them in my room at home.

As a kid, I was totally drawn to the nearby tracks. Although I could not see them from where I lived, I was close enough to hear even the crossing bells from where the nearest road went over the rail line.

In an earlier book (*Freight Weather*, from 2001), I recalled the impact of the presence of those tracks this way:

> Especially at night when there were few other distractions, I could clearly hear the air horn warnings as freight trains approached two distant road crossings ... it was the sound of the railroad night, and it conjured up mysteries that have never left my spirit: I wondered where the trains were going; I imagined their westward routes across the Midwestern plains and pictured far off railroad scenes ...

As is the case with countless other communities around the United States, however, the railroad landscape where I was born and raised changed considerably as the years advanced. In 1968, the iconic New York Central merged with Pennsylvania Railroad and became Penn Central. That experiment did not work out, and over the years, traffic on several of the former NYC routes into Jackson dried up. These lines experienced reduced train frequency before first being taken out of service and were eventually abandoned and removed.

A personal timeline of the metamorphosis impacting the Jackson–Elkhart mainline near my neighborhood reads like this: In 1953, the year I was born, New York Central owned the tracks. When I was fifteen, Penn Central took over the line. Conrail ran the trains when I turned twenty-three. By the time I reached the age of twenty-eight, the route had been taken out of service. At thirty, the rails and ties were being removed.

A short feature from my hometown newspaper, *Jackson Citizen Patriot*, described the ghoulish demise of the Jackson–Elkhart tracks that were central to my years in Michigan. It was dated October 18, 1983, and titled "100 Years of Trains Reach End of Line." The article displayed five photos taken by newspaper staff photographer Bob Keyes, showing crews working for A&K Railroad Materials, a salvage business based in Salt Lake City.

According to the article, forty Michigan workers had begun tearing up 60 miles of track, from Jackson west to Wasepi, in April 1983 and hoped to "finish the job before the first snowfall." It is still heartbreaking to see those photos of rails being lifted and placed on a flatbed truck, and to see ties being stacked to be sold for use in landscaping.

In the article, an unnamed spokesman for Conrail—which inherited the line when it took over Penn Central in 1976—indicated the Interstate Commerce Commission had approved the end of rail service there "because freight trains were no longer using the route."

The photographs in *Northbound Lights* provide a glimpse into some of the changes Michigan and Wisconsin have gone through over the past five decades, with an extra focus on the year 2002 to illustrate how fast the industry has shifted in just the past twenty years. Many of the scenes

MILEPOST 6: Looking to the east in March 1971: A signal tower 6 miles west of the big Penn Central freight yard in Jackson, Michigan, displays an amber aspect, signifying the approach of an eastbound freight train out of Elkhart, Indiana.

COLORFUL CASCADES: Jackson is home to a unique man-made waterfall called "The Cascades," which features cascading water brightly illuminated by an alternating sequence of colored lights. The scenic attraction was one of the highlights of growing up in Jackson ... along with railroad tracks that radiated out of town in eight directions.

in this book reveal the magnitude of the transition in the rail transportation network across this region. Through the harsh lens of time, a busy mainline in one photograph may suddenly transform into a dirt trail in another photo.

I always considered Wisconsin and Michigan to be "sister states." They seem very similar in landscapes, in weather patterns, in the respective states' overall economic focus on agriculture as well as manufacturing, and of course they both possess a strong Great Lakes heritage. The two states also have shared rail links, with mainlines and branchlines in Michigan's Upper Peninsula crossing directly into northern Wisconsin. Most of those lines are now gone, but the memories and heritage remain.

Further, until the 1980s, Wisconsin and Michigan were also linked by a network of railroad car ferries that plowed back and forth across Lake Michigan, forging a rail connection between several port cities (Kewaunee, Manitowoc, and Milwaukee in Wisconsin; Elberta, Ludington, and Muskegon in Michigan). In Michigan, the Ann Arbor Railroad, Chesapeake & Ohio, and Grand Trunk Western operated fleets of car ferries that interchanged traffic with railroads in Wisconsin, including Soo Line, Chicago & NorthWestern, and Green Bay & Western. This direct connection existed for close to a century.

Michigan and Wisconsin are large states. Wisconsin covers 54,310 sq. miles, while Michigan weighs in at a nearly identical 56,804 sq. miles. According to Rand McNally & Company, publisher of *Handy Railroad Atlas of the United States*, Wisconsin had roughly 6,420 miles of railroad tracks operating in the state in 1973, with fourteen different companies providing rail service. That same year, Michigan came in with approximately 6,990 miles of track, with twenty-four active railroad companies.

EIGHT TO THREE: For decades, Jackson—seen here in the winter of 1970—was a major hub for New York Central and later Penn Central railroad operations in southern Michigan, with tracks radiating out of town in seven directions. A branchline of the Grand Trunk Western also came into town. Only four of those eight lines remained by the time Conrail took over the former NYC stronghold in 1976, and as of 2023 only three routes—east to Detroit, west to Chicago via Kalamazoo, and north to Lansing—continue to be active rail corridors.

WEST FROM DETROIT: In December 1970, a Penn Central freight blasts westbound past a spur track at Spring Arbor, Michigan, on its mainline route from Detroit, Michigan, to Elkhart, Indiana, via natural landmarks such as Lime Lake and communities including Jackson, Concord, Union City, Tekonsha, and Three Rivers. Automobiles and auto parts were a major source of freight traffic for Michigan railroads in the 1970s ... and remain so in 2023.

Those numbers have fallen precipitously: In 2022, Wisconsin now has only 3,300 miles of active track, operated by twelve railroads. Michigan logs in with 3,600 miles, handled by twenty-nine different businesses. While the mileage totals are sharply reduced from the levels of the 1970s, that is still a large number of railroads and railroad miles. Accordingly, this book is not geared to be a virtual encyclopedia of every railroad line and every variation in operations, but rather to provide an overview of what has taken place in recent decades. In this book's 140 photographs, approximately eighty-five different communities—mostly small and rural—are featured, and a diverse variety of railroad companies are highlighted.

The transportation revolution reflected in these photographs is striking. Almost all of the railroads whose tracks criss-crossed Michigan and Wisconsin in the 1970s are now gone. Chicago & NorthWestern was merged into Union Pacific. Soo Line (minus the Lake States Transportation Division portion) and Milwaukee Road were absorbed into Canadian Pacific. Green Bay & Western became part of Wisconsin Central, which subsequently came under the ownership of Canadian National. Grand Trunk Western disappeared into parent Canadian National. Chesapeake & Ohio went through significant corporate reprogramming over the years, and today the C&O/Chessie System lines are part of CSX. Penn Central became the nucleus of Conrail, which thrived for more than two decades and then was divided up between Norfolk Southern and CSX. The Ann Arbor Railroad went through several iterations before eventually seeing most of its mileage operated by Great Lakes Central, with the remaining 50 miles being a "shell of itself" shortline still called Ann Arbor Railroad. Escanaba & Lake Superior expanded significantly by taking over tracks previously owned by Milwaukee Road. Detroit & Mackinac's lines became Lake State Railroad. Most recently, in January 2022, Grand Elk Railroad acquired CN's line from Trout Lake to Newberry and Munising in the Upper Peninsula of Michigan. The list goes on and on.

Consider Wisconsin Junction, Wisconsin, as a symbolic case in point regarding alterations in the railroad maps of Wisconsin and Michigan: Two important Soo Line routes once met at this obscure station in the northern Wisconsin woods, which some maps refer to as Argonne. There are two photos in this book taken at Wisconsin Junction in 2002, just a year after Wisconsin Central was taken over by Canadian National.

One photo from Wisconsin Junction faces north at the switch that provided access to or from the old Soo Line east–west route across northern Wisconsin and Michigan's Upper Peninsula. That route was Sault Ste. Marie, Michigan, to Minneapolis–Saint Paul via Trout Lake, Michigan, and Rhinelander, Wisconsin. The second photo looks west on the east–west line, just a few hundred feet from where the tracks cut south. Trains heading south from Wisconsin Junction could go to Milwaukee or Chicago via Black Creek, Oshkosh, and Fond du Lac in Wisconsin.

Wisconsin Junction became part of Wisconsin Central in 1987 and remained quite active. However, once Canadian National purchased Wisconsin Central in 2001, operational changes came fast in the wake of the transaction. Within a few years of the sale to CN, the tracks going south from Wisconsin Junction were removed, and rail service on the east–west route through Wisconsin Junction was discontinued.

In 2023, this once busy junction is now a ghost. The nearest trains are at Rhinelander, 26 miles west of Wisconsin Junction; at Goodman, roughly 27 miles to the east; or at Shawano, 76 miles

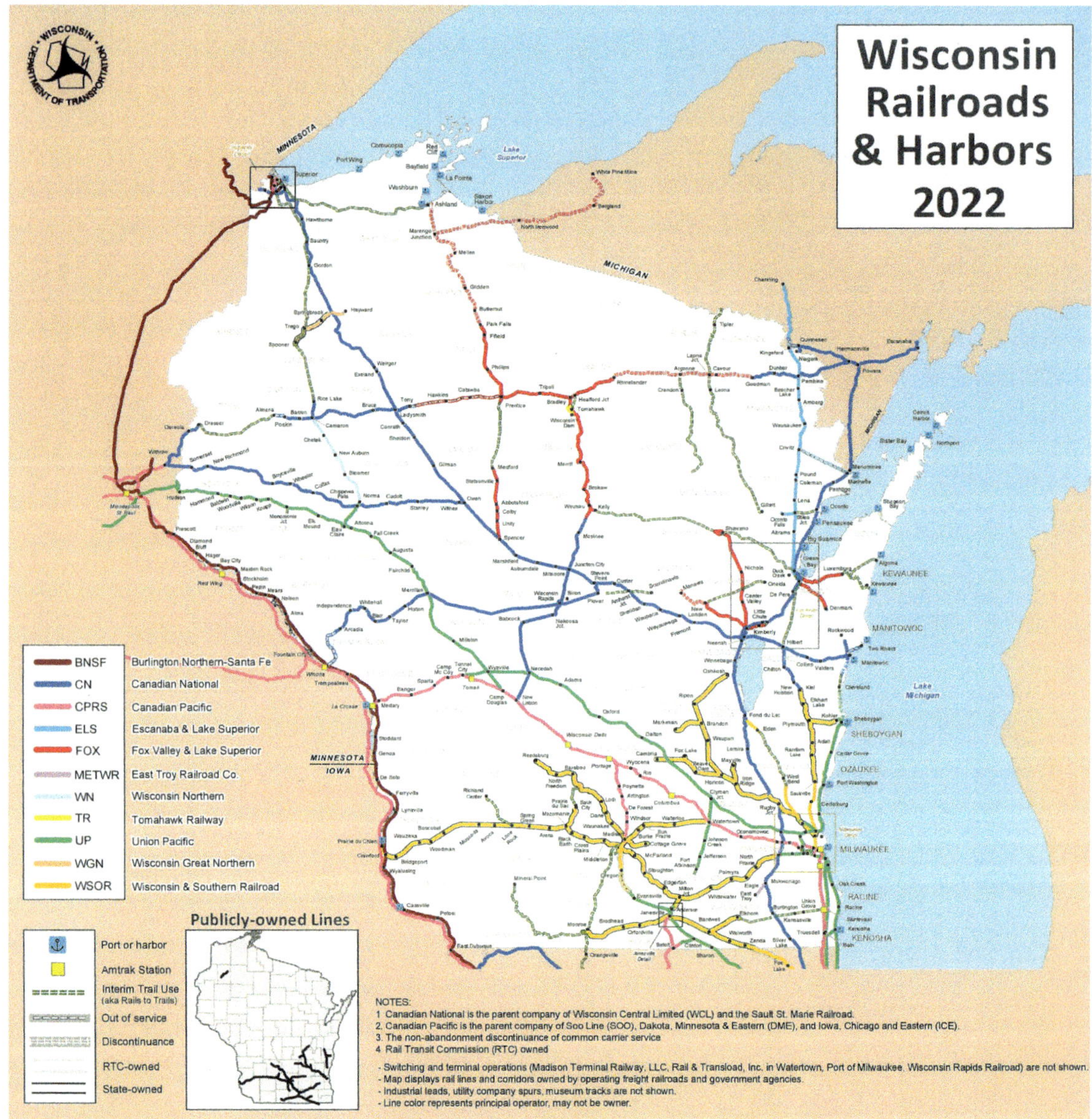

WISCONSIN RAIL LINES: *(Map courtesy of Wisconsin Department of Transportation)*

MICHIGAN RAIL LINES: *(Map courtesy of Michigan Department of Transportation)*

WONDER ISLANDS: Wisconsin, like Michigan, is a land of great scenic beauty. This postcard spotlights the wondrous vistas of land and water found in the Apostle Islands, located in Lake Superior adjacent to the cities of Ashland and Bayfield, near the northwestern edge of the state. (*Author's collection*)

to the south. Goodman continues to be served by CN, while the tracks into Rhinelander and Shawano are now operated by Fox Valley & Lake Superior. There is at least a possibility, however, that new owner FV&LS could reopen the line between Rhinelander and Goodman. The rails are still in place there, but in stretches they are virtually invisible due to nature reclaiming the long-unused corridor. Massive evolutions indeed, with the many abandonments sad to witness.

Here is a poignant memory of what used to be, an observation from Grand Trunk Western tracks in Owosso, Michigan, on July 4, 1974. This is simply a representative "snapshot in time" of operations on the Grand Rapids Subdivision, a GTW route from Durand to Muskegon via St. Johns and Grand Rapids. Back then, the east–west mainline of GTW's Grand Rapids Sub paralleled the Ann Arbor Railroad's mainline for about 11 miles, from Durand through Owosso. The two mainlines were separated only by a short weedy strip of ditch; there were literally just a few yards between the two routes.

I was with my buddy Moon, hanging out along the Ann Arbor tracks on that Independence Day in 1974, but nothing was rolling because the railroad had taken the holiday off. Then, as dusk descended in Owosso, suddenly, there was life on the railroad. We were hoping for AA action, but it was GTW that went to work that July 4 evening: two blue GTW locomotives howled into view, moving fast westbound with just one GTW boxcar and a red GTW caboose.

It was difficult to figure the railroads sometimes. That must have been a hot shipment, or perhaps that's all the traffic GTW was getting in those days and the railroad ran a daily schedule regardless of

LAKE MICHIGAN SUNDOWN: The Frankfort, Michigan, breakwater/lighthouse at dusk on October 19, 2021. Frankfort Harbor was once home base to the Ann Arbor Railroad's car ferry fleet, which, from 1892 until 1982, carried freight cars across the big lake between Michigan and Wisconsin.

the tonnage. That was a sight to see, however, and I sure wish I had carried a camera with me then to record it, as the Grand Rapids Sub was abandoned in the 1990s.

Here are two additional vignettes of "ancient" rail operations worthy of sharing. These tales, taken straight from my journal writings in 1979, spotlight some of the titanic transformations in Michigan and Wisconsin over the past several decades.

First, from St. Ignace, Michigan, at Soo Line's car ferry slip where *Chief Wawatam* docked for loading and unloading. *Chief Wawatam* was a 1911-era, coal-fired steamer that moved railroad cars across the Straits of Mackinac—St. Ignace to Mackinaw City—to directly connect the railroads of Michigan's Upper Peninsula and Lower Peninsula (this unique operation died in 1984):

> We watch the car ferry "Chief Wawatam" being loaded. The ferry makes its three-hour round trip run twice on this Monday, carrying a total of 35 cars over to Mackinaw City. Yet twice it comes back with an empty belly—no traffic coming back north! Odd.

Indeed, why was there so much freight going south that July day in 1979, and nothing coming north?

Here is a strange story from that 1979 summer of travel. This was on Chicago & NorthWestern, on the railroad's route from Powers, Michigan, south to Marinette, Wisconsin. Moon and I were in Powers early in the morning; we'd come down on a very slow C&NW train from Escanaba, where all the freight cars on our train were set out. Soon, however, another C&NW freight came in from Iron Mountain and traded cars at Powers—a "middle of nowhere" station—with the train from Escanaba.

> After leaving Powers on the C&NW route heading south, the train moved much faster than on the Escanaba to Powers segment. In fact, it is so fast that safety concerns seemed to be scoffed at. This is what we witnessed: There are pulp logs sticking out from the sides of several gondolas on our southbound train. It appears the shaking of the train has caused the logs to vibrate out of their neat stacks to the point where they are hanging over the edge of the gondolas by several feet. Not a safe situation.
>
> When we crossed a bridge, the logs strike the steel beams of the bridge and go flying in all directions. Incredible the railroad could let this happen. It could easily cause a derailment. Fortunately for us, the gondolas with the unruly logs are behind us by about 30 cars. We braced ourselves for a derailment when we saw what was happening. At least the biggest mess is behind us, so if there is a wreck, we reasoned, our car will probably stay on the track; we will just have to hold on tight as the train goes into emergency.
>
> Twice we watch logs literally explode into the steel braces of different trestles, and at one road crossing I see a motorist hurriedly back up as the flying, tumbling logs are coming his way. This is madness. I can't believe the railroad would routinely allow logs to shake loose to become such a safety and derailment hazard. Surely the crew is aware of what's transpiring? We can see it, so we have to assume the guy in the caboose or the crew in the engine can see the same thing.

Thankfully, that train did not derail, but what we saw that summer day in 1979 was clearly no way to run a railroad.

As an artistic emphasis, I have always admired the lines and angles of tracks and trains and the way the light plays along the metal surfaces. I also appreciate the rainbow of colors, the sense of motion—physical and spatial—and how photographs taken across the years can capture the contrasts of history.

Taken as a package, the photographs and descriptive captions presented in *Northbound Lights* attempt to capture the wonder of seeing a distant, oncoming headlamp and not knowing for certain what kind of train is eventually going to heave into view. The photos in this book of obscure junctions and trains moving to all points over the landscapes of Wisconsin and Michigan hold a special poignancy, especially remembering how much more activity there once was on many of these rail lines.

Numerous rural stations—wonderful places with names such as Black Creek, Reed City, Thompsonville, and Marengo Junction—do not see any rail traffic these days, even though they once were interchange locations where two railroads intersected. Too many small towns no longer have railroad tracks slicing along the edge of the business district, and once shiny spur tracks into factories or agricultural warehouses or lumber wholesalers are rusted over.

Yet in these scenes, the heritage and spirit of the railroad lives on. *Northbound Lights* reflects the art and magic of the forever changing network of steel rails across Wisconsin and Michigan.

D. C. Jesse Burkhardt
October 8, 2022

1

On the Fast Mainlines

FAST TRACK: A Canadian National freight appears to be rising out of the tall trackside vegetation as it heads east at Junction City, Wisconsin.

OVER THE RIVER: In July 2002, a Canadian Pacific coal train crosses a bridge over the Wisconsin River as it powers southeast at Wisconsin Dells, Wisconsin, on what was once Milwaukee Road's primary east–west mainline across the state.

HERITAGE PAINT: Canadian Pacific has repainted several of its locomotives—including SD70 #7011, seen here on February 23, 2021—in paint schemes from an earlier era to honor the railroad's history. CP, which reaches coast to coast in Canada, took over numerous former Soo Line and Milwaukee Road routes in Wisconsin and Michigan in 1990.

MARCELLUS TRAFFIC: At Marcellus, Michigan, in July 2014, a long freight train with a diverse mix of cargo moves westward on Canadian National's ex-Grand Trunk Western mainline between Port Huron, Michigan, and Chicago, Illinois.

THREE-WAY STATION: Routes of three active railroads converge at the lonely and obscure rural crossing known as Diann, Michigan. This view is facing west on what was once Detroit, Toledo & Ironton's main route between Detroit, Michigan, and Ironton, Ohio. In the contemporary configuration here, a north–south Ann Arbor Railroad line crosses Canadian National (tracks east of Diann) and Indiana & Ohio Railroad (tracks west of Diann).

MILWAUKEE SOO: Soo Line caboose #30 and ex-Milwaukee Road GP40 #2066—working together in local duty at La Crosse, Wisconsin—rest in the yard as the sun begins to set in the summer of 2014. Soo Line purchased Milwaukee Road in 1985.

WYEVILLE MAIN: Union Pacific's east-west mainline between Milwaukee, Wisconsin, and St. Paul, Minnesota, passes through rural Wyeville, Wisconsin, once a crossing of two Chicago & NorthWestern routes. Much has changed over the decades: The tracks are now under Union Pacific ownership, and the physical crossing of the two ex-C&NW lines has been removed. This scene is looking east on October 18, 2021, from where trains once clattered across the intersecting diamond. The now-superfluous crossing gate is still in place.

TAKING OVER: April 30, 2005: Norfolk Southern motors (GP38-2 #5212 and C40-9s #8824 and #9662) idle in the former Conrail freight yard in Jackson, Michigan, awaiting orders to move freight. NS took over operations on this east–west Detroit-Chicago property in 1999, in the wake of Conrail's demise.

RED LIGHTS ON THE HORIZON: On a cold day in November 2013, two red signal lights shine in the distance at Emmett, Michigan, on Canadian National's former Grand Trunk Western route that runs west from Port Huron. GTW, a longtime subsidiary of CN, was fully merged into the CN network in 1991.

SAFETY FIRST: A metal sign next to Canadian Pacific's double-tracked mainline at Columbus, Wisconsin, warns travelers and pedestrians to pay attention around the tracks here. In addition to being a busy freight route, Columbus also sees a daily round trip from Amtrak's *Empire Builder*, a passenger train operating in the Chicago–Seattle corridor.

DOUBLE-TRACK SPEEDWAY: Canadian Pacific's busy Milwaukee–Minneapolis mainline stretches to the western horizon near Lewiston, Wisconsin.

CORNFIELD RUSH: Amtrak's daily *Empire Builder* slices eastward through central Wisconsin on its run from Seattle to Chicago, passing cornfields and a classic John Deere tractor being overtaken by vegetation. The passenger train is just a few miles away from Portage, Wisconsin, its next station stop.

DUELING WESTBOUNDS: A Canadian Pacific crew boards a westbound auto parts train (*top photo*) in Portage on July 19, 2002. Before the freight can start pulling, however, the crew must wait for Amtrak's westbound *Empire Builder* to arrive at the station. Portage is one of six Wisconsin cities served by the long-distance *Empire Builder*.

ROAD POWER: Three pristine motors rest on the ready track at the edge of Canadian Pacific's extensive freight yard in Portage in 2002. Serviced and ready to pull a long train on the railroad's mainline between Milwaukee and La Crosse, Wisconsin, are CP GP38-2 #4422, Soo Line GP38-2 #4401, and CP GP40 #4602. In a newer, cherry red paint scheme (*bottom photo*), Soo Line SD40-2 #6054 is set to pull west out of the Portage yard.

HARSH REFUELING: A crewman is refueling CSX GP40-3 #6536, power for the day's local, at Plymouth, Michigan, on December 26, 2016. A hi-rail vehicle inspecting the tracks in the soupy weather passes by on the mainline. (*Photo by Peter Hayes*)

STILL IN PORT HURON: Despite abandoning its two mainline routes into Port Huron, Michigan, over recent decades, CSX maintains a presence in the city, which is an active industrial area and a rail gateway to Canada. In November 2013, CSX GP38-2 #2613 and a sister CSX motor are busy switching cars in an outlying freight yard.

HOLLAND DUSK: The view to the north from the depot platform at Holland, Michigan, as night descends on the tracks, the signal towers, and the scenic tourist town in June 2017. The CSX-owned rails here are part of the railroad's important route between Chicago, Illinois, and Grand Rapids, Michigan. Amtrak's *Pere Marquette* passenger train between those points also makes a daily visit to Holland.

BUSY YARD: Since 1897, Ludington, Michigan, had been first Pere Marquette Railway's and later Chesapeake & Ohio's base of operations for its fleet of Lake Michigan car ferries, which moved freight cars between Michigan and Wisconsin. With the ending of ferry service in the 1980s, it seemed that the railroad route into Ludington might become an abandonment candidate. But Dow Chemical's calcium chloride production facility in Ludington is a major industrial shipper, as this 2002 look at the congested CSX freight yard in town makes clear. CSX GP38s #2640 and #2568 are tackling this day's switching assignments.

CHESSIE CAT: Chessie System caboose #903158, with the wonderful "cat on a pillow" logo emblazoned on its side, assists with the railroad's switching operations in Ludington. The Chessie System, successor to Chesapeake & Ohio, was created in 1973 as Chessie became the parent of C&O, Baltimore & Ohio, and Western Maryland. The Chessie era lasted only from 1973 until 1980, when CSX became the new corporate parent.

GOOD TRACK GONE: Heat radiates off the ex-Grand Trunk Western mainline from Owosso, Michigan, to Grand Rapids and Muskegon through St. Johns and Ionia in this westward view. The route west of Owosso was abandoned and removed in the early 1990s. The GTW's slogan was "The Good Track Road."

RETURN TO FLINT: Once common, stencils painted on the sides of freight cars informed railroad workers where to return empties after they had reached their destination and been unloaded. This Grand Trunk Western boxcar, photographed in February 1990, was slated to be routed back to Flint, Michigan, a key industrial center served by GTW.

CANADIAN COMPETITORS: Working solo, Canadian Pacific #8728 hauls auto carriers and containers (*top photo*) westbound past the triple towers at snowy Duplainville, Wisconsin, on March 11, 2019. Just over an hour later, CP's historical rival Canadian National rocks north across CP's high speed mainline here with a container train of its own. (*Both photos by Peter Hayes*)

CHANGING OF THE GUARD: Restored New York Central caboose #17965 (*top*) shows off its proud heritage in the Old Town area of Ypsilanti, Michigan. New York Central merged with Pennsylvania Railroad in 1968 to create Penn Central, which operated rail lines across Michigan and many other states. However, just eight years later, in 1976, a new carrier—Conrail—was created to take over the struggling Penn Central system. In the bottom photo, Conrail bay window caboose #24039 rests alone in the railroad's yard in Jackson, waiting for its next assignment.

DEPOT TOWN: The siding and spur tracks alongside Norfolk Southern's ex-New York Central mainline through the Old Town business district of Ypsilanti no longer serve a purpose and are being removed in this scene from November 2013. The defunct passenger depot on the right does not host passengers, as Ypsilanti—home to Eastern Michigan University—is not an Amtrak stop, but this route in the Detroit–Chicago corridor remains busy with freight traffic and several daily Amtrak runs.

WISCONSIN DELLS: Canadian Pacific's route through Wisconsin Dells, Wisconsin—the former Milwaukee Road mainline between Milwaukee and Minneapolis–Saint Paul—is a busy property, as exemplified by these comings and goings on July 19, 2002. *Top photo*: A mixed manifest is heading northwest behind solo CP motor #9534. Not long after this train has passed, a train rumbles southeast past the Wisconsin Dells Amtrak station platform on its run to Milwaukee with mixed merchandise (*bottom photo*). A former Milwaukee Road locomotive, GP40 #2016, leads the train. The Milwaukee Road identity of #2016 has been painted over, somewhat crudely, and the unit has been relettered for new owner Soo Line, which merged the Milwaukee Road system in 1985.

MICHIGAN HAULER: Cutting through the scenic summer landscape at Caffey, Michigan, on June 25, 1999, a mixed freight is headed westbound on Wisconsin Central's key east–west route in Michigan's Upper Peninsula. The long train, moving mostly forest products, is on its way from Sault Ste. Marie to Gladstone, Michigan, powered by WC SD45 #6620, Algoma Central F9B #1761, and WC GP40 #3025. *Bottom photo:* Five days later, on June 30, 1999, WC's daily hauler is rolling west near Manistique, Michigan, behind a similar mixture of road motors: WC SD45 #7495, Algoma Central FP9 #1753, and WC GP40 #3005.

FRIENDLY CROSSING: A Canadian National freight blasts southbound across the former Soo Line main at Junction City, Wisconsin, on July 18, 2002. The train, headed by SD40-2 #6256 and GP40 #3137—both lettered for CN-controlled Illinois Central—is rolling on an ex-Milwaukee Road route linking Wausau and Wisconsin Rapids. Mergers have slashed competition across the Midwest, and the routes that cross here are both now under the ownership of Canadian National. Note the train's loads of pulpwood logs (*bottom photo*) being hauled in Algoma Central gondolas. Algoma Central, which serves the Canadian province of Ontario, is also controlled by CN, which inherited the shortline when it purchased the 2,850-mile Wisconsin Central in 2001.

APPROACHING: Headlights appear in the distance as another CN freight train approaches busy Junction City, this one from the west. Note the roller coaster profile along this stretch of track.

WESTBOUND TO WINONA: In this colorful postcard scene from August 1977, a long Green Bay & Western freight is ready to power westward out of GB&W's yard complex in Green Bay, Wisconsin, bound for Winona, Minnesota. Much of the 250-mile east–west mainline of the former "Green Bay Route" has since been abandoned. *(Author's collection)*

BOAT TRACKS: A rainy-day view facing west in August 1997 at MP 30.3 on the former Green Bay & Western mainline between Green Bay and Kewaunee in Wisconsin. Until the 1980s, these tracks hosted daily "Boat Trains" to and from Kewaunee that interchanged traffic with Ann Arbor Railroad and Chesapeake & Ohio car ferries. In January 1998, Fox Valley & Western Railroad—a shortline that had taken over this route—filed a petition to abandon the segment east from Luxemburg to Kewaunee, roughly 17 miles.

CONRAIL QUALITY: Conrail was formed in 1976 in the wake of the collapse of Penn Central, and it brought stability to the mess Penn Central and several other bankrupt railroads in the region had become. In Michigan, Conrail's role serving the automobile industry was vital, as the railroad moved auto parts and finished cars and trucks across the nation. Conrail operated until 1999, when Norfolk Southern and CSX forged a deal to divide up Conrail's network of track.

SUNRISE TRAIN: Amtrak's daily early morning southbound train between Grand Rapids, Michigan, and Chicago—the *Pere Marquette*—crosses the Kalamazoo River on CSX rails at New Richmond, Michigan, in July 2013.

FRESH CREW BOARDING: A crew member climbs aboard the lead locomotive on Amtrak's westbound *Empire Builder*, which is preparing to leave Minot, North Dakota, as it continues its westward run on July 20, 2002. The *Empire Builder* provides daily service across the heart of Wisconsin on its 2,200-mile route between Chicago and Seattle/Portland, with Wisconsin station stops in Milwaukee, Columbus, Portage, Wisconsin Dells, Tomah, and La Crosse.

OBSOLETE LINEUP: An outdated passenger train schedule board greets travelers in the Jackson train station in 1992. Even then, the Grand Rapids Branch no longer existed, while the Saginaw Branch was freight only and the rails came to an end less than 40 miles away in Lansing—nearly 70 miles south of Saginaw. In 2023, Amtrak's *Wolverine* provides three daily round-trips in and out of Jackson, moving passengers east and west between Detroit and Chicago.

AMTRAK MIDWEST: Amtrak's routes in the Midwest, as shown in the Amtrak System Timetable effective January 11, 2016.

HISTORIC ROOTS: Amtrak's passenger train stop in Ann Arbor, Michigan, is adjacent to this ornate former Michigan Central depot, built in 1886. Amtrak's Chicago–Detroit trains pass through Ann Arbor several times a day on this former New York Central line, now operated by Norfolk Southern.

DOUBLE DIAMONDS: BNSF's east–west mainline between Chicago and Seattle crosses the Canadian Pacific mainline at Soo Tower in North Dakota. This route is part of BNSF's transcontinental mainline between the Chicago-Milwaukee region of the Midwest and Seattle-Portland on the West Coast. As the name of the junction implies, Soo Line once owned CP Rail's north–south route that crosses here. BNSF's track is former Great Northern Railway.

EAST FROM SOO TOWER: A BNSF stack train rolls eastward over CP Rail's mainline at Soo Tower, North Dakota, on July 2, 1999. Trains on this route cut across western Wisconsin on a mainline that directly parallels the Mississippi River for roughly 250 miles.

DOWN AT THE STATION: A northbound Canadian Pacific freight holds at the signal tower next to the aging Milwaukee Road depot in Hastings, Minnesota, directly across the Mississippi River from Wisconsin, on July 1, 1999. Leading the waiting freight are two vintage engines displaying their fading heritage: an ex-Milwaukee Road unit (GP40 #2011) and an ex-Soo Line unit (GP38-2 #4423), both in their traditional 1970s paint schemes. The northbounder is waiting for a Canadian Pacific stack train to come south (*bottom photo*) over a single-track bridge across the river here. Soo Line merged Milwaukee Road in 1985, and then, in 1990, CP took full control of Soo Line.

NORTHERN REACH: Almost all of BNSF's trackage in Wisconsin runs along the iconic Mississippi River on the state's western border, a route that is a key part of the railroad's mainline between Chicago and Seattle. However, BNSF also has a stretch of track in the northwestern corner of Wisconsin that provides the far-ranging transcontinental carrier with access to the busy shipping and industrial districts of Superior, Wisconsin, and Duluth, Minnesota.

EAST TO DETROIT: Norfolk Southern's vital double-track mainline (former Norfolk & Western, and Wabash before that) slices through Milan, Michigan, a small town along the railroad's Chicago–Detroit corridor. Milan is also an interchange point with shortline Ann Arbor Railroad. This view looks east toward Detroit, which is less than 40 miles from Milan.

LATE SNOW: The calendar shows it is early May—May 10, 1991, to be precise—yet significant snow remains on the ground as winter holds on, providing a striking contrast as vivid red Soo Line and CP Rail engines power into East Lansing, Michigan, running on CSX mainline rails between Detroit and Grand Rapids. (*Photo by Dennis Schmidt*)

CSX ON BNSF: In July 2014, a long westbound oil train led by multiple CSX motors thunders past the day's eastbound *Empire Builder*, which has paused on BNSF rails at the Minot, North Dakota, Amtrak station before continuing on its way to Minneapolis, Milwaukee, and Chicago.

2

The Backwater Branches

NORTHBOUND REFLECTIONS: Headlights on a northbound Huron & Eastern freight light up the tracks as a train bound for Bad Axe, Michigan, comes around a distant bend.

RANDVILLE IN THE RAIN: On July 17, 2002, covered hoppers on a siding wait for a call to return to service during a refreshing rainstorm at Randville in Michigan's Upper Peninsula. This view is looking south along Escanaba & Lake Superior tracks previously owned by Milwaukee Road.

HEADLIGHTS SOUTH: A short train on Tuscola & Saginaw Bay Railroad's route between Petoskey and Cadillac rolls into Manton, Michigan, on a snowy day in October 1992. The southbound is powered by GP35 #390, still in its old Ann Arbor Railroad colors.

REPAINT CANDIDATE: In fading paint, Tuscola & Saginaw Bay GP35 #393 rests on a spur track near Traverse City, Michigan, on July 15, 2002. The ex-Ann Arbor locomotive was built in 1964.

GREEN BAY LOCAL: Escanaba & Lake Superior Railroad's northbound local out of Green Bay rambles over ex-Milwaukee Road trackage behind SD9 #1222 as it nears Crivitz, Wisconsin, in the summer of 2002. SD9 #1222 was built in 1955 for Minnesota-based Reserve Mining, a company that mined taconite.

BACKWATER BRANCH: Stiles Junction, Wisconsin, July 17, 2002: The top photo is a view to the north on track now belonging to Escanaba & Lake Superior. Signal towers next to the abandoned station here once protected a north-south Milwaukee Road line against an intersecting Chicago & NorthWestern branch between Oconto and Oconto Falls, 14 miles. If you can find them in the tall grass and weeds (*bottom photo*), the rails leading west to Oconto Falls are shiny with use, surprising given the neglected condition of this backwater junction. Lumber and farming businesses at Oconto Falls still use the railroad, but now the branch goes just 5 miles, from Stiles Junction to Oconto Falls. The tracks east from Stiles Junction to Oconto were removed long ago.

VIEW FROM TROUT LAKE: Wisconsin Central's freight yard at Trout Lake, Michigan, is quiet in this westward view from 1999. In the Soo Line era, this station on an east–west mainline was also home to a local going south to St. Ignace to interchange traffic coming across the Straits of Mackinac on the car ferry *Chief Wawatam*. The line to St. Ignace was abandoned in 1986, but Trout Lake remains active in 2023 with Canadian National and Grand Elk Railroad operating here.

COPPER RUN: A westbound train on Wisconsin Central's White Pine Subdivision rocks slowly through Thomaston, Michigan, on June 23, 1999. The train is returning from its thrice-weekly trip to a copper mine at White Pine, Michigan. Powered by a single GP40, WC #3023, the long train is headed toward Marengo Junction in Wisconsin.

SWITCH LEFT: Tracks of regional railroad Great Lakes Central switch off from the main at Walton Junction, Michigan. In this scene from June 2011, the rails are lined for traffic to head northwest to Traverse City, about 25 miles away. Trains going due north from this remote junction would eventually end up in Petoskey, roughly 75 miles up the tracks. The route is a remnant of an ex-Pennsylvania Railroad line that ran between Grand Rapids and Mackinaw City.

120 MILES: Concrete milepost markers from the New York Central era are still doing their job decades after they were installed in this trackside scene at Gaylord, Michigan. The "BC" stands for Bay City, and the "120" means this location is 120 miles north of Bay City, where the route through Gaylord and on north to Cheboygan and Mackinaw City originated. Lake State Railway now operates this track, but the rails north of Gaylord were removed in the early 1990s.

TANKS ON THE MOVE: Escanaba & Lake Superior SD9 #1221 and GP38 #400 pull a long line of tank cars slowly south at Beecher, Wisconsin, on July 17, 2002. The train is headed toward Green Bay on the old Milwaukee Road north–south route between Green Bay and Iron Mountain, Michigan, which E&LS purchased in 1982. The SD9 doing the pulling on this run was built for Reserve Mining in 1955, while the GP38 was built in 1970 for Penn Central.

HIAWATHA SERVICE: This artistic logo was the symbol of Milwaukee Road's "Hiawatha" passenger trains, regional runs that originated in Chicago and served several of the railroad's routes in the upper Midwest. Included in the lineup was the daily *Chippewa-Hiawatha*, which traveled a 315-mile route between Chicago and Ontonagon, Michigan, a town on the southern shore of Lake Superior. The *Chippewa-Hiawatha* went by way of Milwaukee and Green Bay in Wisconsin and Iron Mountain and Channing in Michigan. It operated from 1937 until 1960.

HEADLAMPS THROUGH THE GREEN: Heavy vegetation slowly encroaches onto the roadbed near Coleman, Wisconsin, as approaching headlights announce the arrival of an E&LS freight rolling northbound about halfway between Green Bay and Pembine.

CRIVITZ YARD: Escanaba & Lake Superior crew members meet in the freight yard in Crivitz, Wisconsin, to discuss the day's operations (or plans for fishing later) before boarding their respective trains in 2002. Crivitz is a small community near the Peshtigo River and Lake Noquebay. The town was served by Milwaukee Road until the 1980s, when E&LS purchased the bankrupt carrier's north–south line between Green Bay, Wisconsin, and Republic, Michigan. Another line branches southeast from Crivitz to Marinette, Wisconsin, but as of 2023, the 21-mile route to Marinette is out of service.

STEVENS POINT TO PLOVER: A crew out of nearby Stevens Point works with Wisconsin Central SW1500 #1566 in an industrial area of Plover, Wisconsin, on July 12, 2002. For many years, Plover served as a key interchange point for Soo Line and Green Bay & Western, but the importance of the station dropped off in the 1980s as the GB&W lost its ferry routes and traffic fell.

SHOWING THE FLAG: Although the Green Bay & Western Railroad had not existed for nearly a decade when this photo was taken in 2002, GB&W boxcars on an active business spur in Kingsford, Michigan, continue to display their proud heritage.

NO LINES REMAIN: Ex-Soo Line GP30 #719 and Wisconsin Central GP35 #2555 lead a northbound freight into Ashland, Wisconsin, at 9 a.m. on a wet June day in 1999. The bottom photo shows the proximity of the active line to the long-ago abandoned spur track leading to ore docks on Lake Superior. This northern Wisconsin town was once served by three railroads—Chicago & NorthWestern, Soo Line, and Burlington Northern—but in 2023, trains no longer call on Ashland, as service has been discontinued from Park Falls north to Ashland, roughly 60 miles.

LIGHTS OUT AT THREE RIVERS: October 25, 2021: The bright colors of autumn leaves contrast with a rusting and aging signal tower at Cowling siding outside Three Rivers, Michigan, on the ex-Conrail line between Grand Rapids, Michigan, and Elkhart, Indiana. This route is now operated by shortline Grand Elk Railroad.

TRACK NEEDS WORK: Headlights heave into view on a shaky stretch of branchline track near Carsonville, Michigan, as a Huron & Eastern Railway freight rocks slowly northbound on what was previously a Chesapeake & Ohio line from Saginaw and Bad Axe to Port Huron. In 1986, Huron & Eastern purchased C&O's track from Kinde south to Croswell, 52 miles, where the line now terminates.

BAD AXE BOUND: Huron & Eastern GP38 #2025 backs toward its train (*top photo*) at Croswell, Michigan, as it readies to take ten cars north to Bad Axe, Michigan, on a bitterly cold afternoon in November 2013. Huron & Eastern serves agricultural shippers in Croswell, a small town 27 miles north of Port Huron and a few miles from the Lake Huron shoreline. *Bottom photo*: A few miles north of Croswell, with dusk descending on the area, the train cuts across a dirt road as it settles in for the 43-mile run from Croswell to Bad Axe. Huron & Eastern operates a total of 395 miles of track in Michigan.

STOVEPIPE SMOKE: On a sunny December day in 1980, the crew of Ann Arbor Railroad System caboose #2834 has the stove going strong as their train passes through snowy Cadillac, Michigan. (*Photo by Dennis Schmidt*)

MIDDLETON MORNING: In this postcard scene, a Milwaukee Road crew working with SD10 #555 enjoys winter railroading on a cold morning in Middleton, Wisconsin, as they switch out cars at the town's industrial park in February 1982. Middleton is located on a former mainline route between Madison and Prairie du Chien. (*Photo by Rod Kreunen*)

ALCO SMOKER: Minnesota Commercial Railroad's ex-Canadian Pacific RS18 #81 pours out its trademark black smoke as it works in St. Paul, Minnesota, on June 20, 1999. Minnesota Commercial is a terminal railroad with a locomotive roster that includes several Alco engines previously in service with Green Bay & Western.

SCENIC TOURS: For a brief few years beginning in 1989, Michigan's Leelanau Scenic Railroad operated excursion trains from its base in Traverse City, seen here in October 1992, to Suttons Bay, about 15 miles. The tourist trains, pulled by a former C&O NW2 switch engine, traveled on the southern portion of an ex-Chesapeake & Ohio branch that once connected Traverse City and Northport.

TRAIL MARKER: Leelanau Scenic Railroad ended operations in 1995, but the excursion business left behind ex-C&O bay window caboose #2938 just north of Traverse City. The caboose, pictured here in April 2005, has since been repainted bright yellow. It rests alongside the Leelanau Trail, which was created out of remnants of the abandoned C&O line that went north to Northport.

TURNING TO TOURISM: With the need for freight service declining and tourism playing a central role in northern Michigan's economy, entrepreneurs stepped up with hopes of enticing tourists to ride the rails. In 1996, the Grand Traverse Dinner Train launched out of Traverse City, using the former C&O depot as its headquarters. In this August 1997 scene, a brightly painted train idles at the station. Dinner train excursions ended in 2005, and the old depot was later transformed into a brewery. The brewery's slogan, quite appropriately, is "Ales by the Rails."

CAMERON STOP: A Wisconsin Central eastbound local led by GP35 #2553 nears Cameron, Wisconsin, as it makes its way east with ten cars on June 21, 1999. A stop sign and gate protects WC's east–west line here from north–south traffic on a neglected ex-Chicago & NorthWestern route out of Eau Claire, Wisconsin. The WC track is a former Soo Line mainline between St. Paul, Minnesota, and Sault Ste. Marie, Michigan, sections of which have been abandoned. When this scene was captured, the tracks terminated at Almena, a few miles west of Cameron. C&NW's old northbound route also has fallen on hard times: The line that once reached all the way to Superior, Wisconsin, now comes to an end in Rice Lake, just 7 miles north of Cameron.

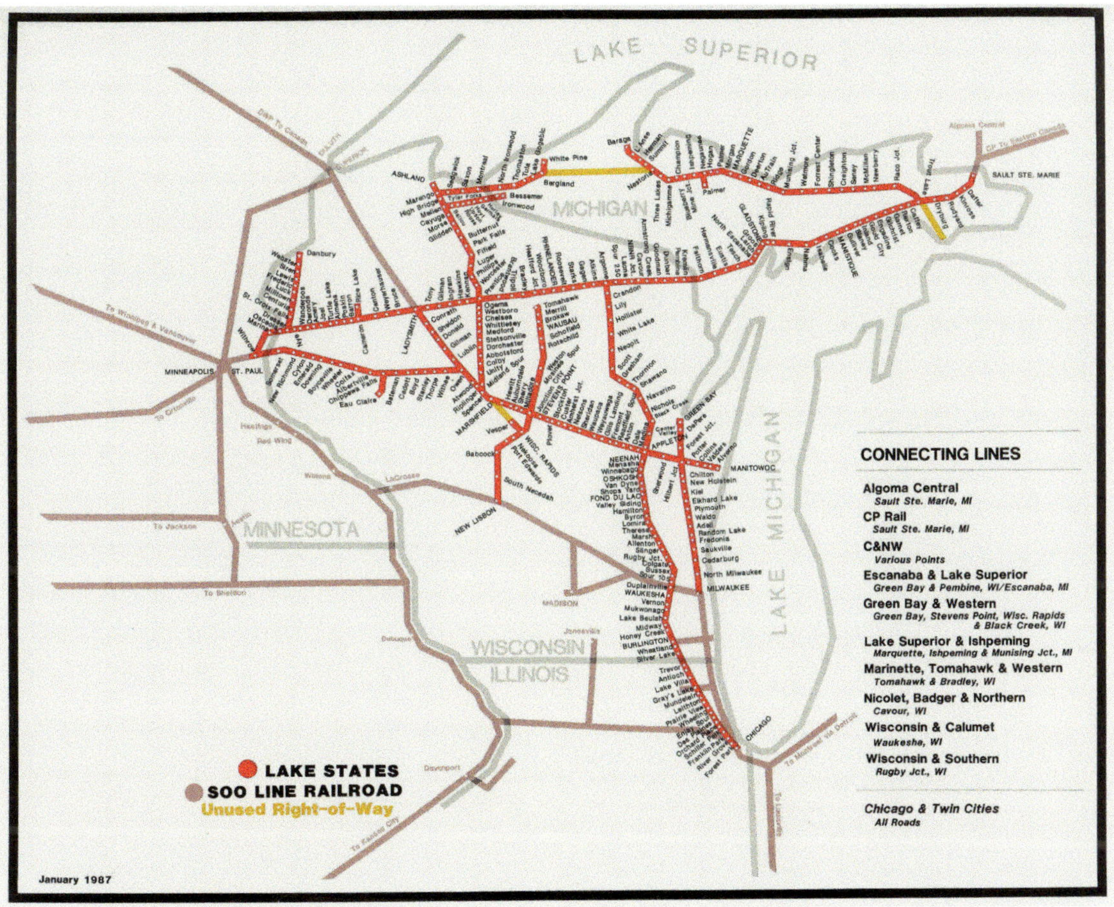

SOO LINE SPINOFF: In early 1986, Soo Line Railroad created the Lake States Transportation Division, a roughly 2,000-mile network. These routes were carved out of Soo Line after the Interstate Commerce Commission ordered the railroad to divest lines in the region to preserve rail competition in the wake of Soo Line's 1985 acquisition of Milwaukee Road. The era of the Lake States Division was fleeting: In 1987, the entire division was purchased by newly created regional carrier Wisconsin Central, which in turn was bought by Canadian National in 2001.

HILBERT JUNCTION, WEST & EAST: The view in July 2002 looking west (*top photo*) and east (*bottom photo*) at Hilbert Junction, Wisconsin, where the rails of Soo Line and Milwaukee Road once crossed. Soo Line went east through here to Manitowoc, Wisconsin, and west toward Stevens Point and beyond. From 1987 until 2001, Wisconsin Central owned this line. In 2023, the old Soo Line route into Manitowoc is operated by Canadian National.

HILBERT JUNCTION, NORTH & SOUTH: Facing north (*top photo*) along CN's ex-Milwaukee Road mainline that once linked Green Bay and Milwaukee. The barrier was in place to protect the east–west route in and out of Manitowoc, a route served by Canadian National since 2001. The tracks are out of service north of Hilbert Junction, but a CN branch runs south (*bottom photo*) from Hilbert to New Holstein, Wisconsin, about 15 miles away.

SOUTHBOUND HOPPERS: In the summer of 2002, Wisconsin Central GP40 #3024 pulls a cut of cars south along an ex-Milwaukee Road line at Chilton, Wisconsin.

HAYWARD SWITCH: A Wisconsin Central freight behind WC SD45 #6556 awaits a fresh crew at Hayward Junction, Wisconsin, on June 21, 1999.

ON THE PLATFORM: The view facing north (*top photo*) from the depot platform at Pembine, Wisconsin, on a hot and muggy July 17, 2002. At Pembine, the former Milwaukee Road tracks between Iron Mountain, Michigan, and Green Bay, Wisconsin, crossed the former Soo Line main from St. Paul, Minnesota, to Sault Ste. Marie, Michigan. In 2023, the Escanaba & Lake Superior operates the north–south line, while Canadian National operates the east–west trackage. *Bottom photo:* Looking east, the old Soo Line station marks the intersection of the two railroads. The east–west trackage here is no longer a mainline: Rail service now comes to an end just 20 miles west of Pembine at Goodman, Wisconsin.

AUTUMN TOUR: Surrounded by amazing fall colors, a Great Lakes Central freight hammers south at McBain, Michigan—a small town between Clare and Cadillac—on October 22, 2021. GP35s #390 and #386 lead the way. Great Lakes Central was created in March 2006 and now operates approximately 400 miles of track in Michigan. *(Photo by Peter Hayes)*

WORKING THE YARD: On the day after Christmas in 2018, two Lake State Railway trains are working in Bay City, Michigan. Lake State GP40 #1166 is putting its train together in the yard, while GP40-2 #805 is switching an industrial spur. The 375-mile Lake State Railway was created in 1992 when the company acquired the northeastern Michigan routes that had been owned by Detroit & Mackinac Railway. *(Photo by Peter Hayes)*

DIAMOND DAYS: Looking north toward the Great Lakes Central/CSX diamond at Ann Pere, Michigan, in July 2014. Ann Pere, directly south of the city of Howell, is an active transfer point between the two railroads. The CSX east–west line here runs between Detroit and Grand Rapids via the capital city of Lansing, while the GLC route operates from Osmer (just north of Ann Arbor) north to Petoskey by way of Cadillac.

DAILY SERVICE: The scene at Interlochen, Michigan, in the summer of 1971, when trains still operated daily in both directions. This is a southwestward view of the Chesapeake & Ohio line between Petoskey and Manistee via Traverse City, which was abandoned in 1982. Traffic on the line declined rapidly following the closure of the massive Penn-Dixie cement plant near Petoskey in 1981.

C&O STATIONS: The view to the north (*top photo*) at Grant, Michigan, on the old C&O line from Grand Rapids to Ludington. In 2002, the town retained much of its trackside railroad heritage, illustrated by the old water tower and warehouse buildings. In 1997 (*bottom photo*), this scene is looking west at Walhalla, Michigan, a key junction point on the same ex-C&O route. From Walhalla, trains could continue north to get to Manistee, Traverse City, and Petoskey, or cut west 16 miles to Ludington, which for many decades was home base for C&O's Lake Michigan car ferry fleet. In 2023, the tracks go north from Walhalla only as far as Manistee, another 27 miles up the line.

400 FEET AHEAD: Wisconsin Junction, Wisconsin, in 2002: Two important Soo Line routes once met at this obscure station in the northern Wisconsin woods. The top photo faces north at the switch that provided access to Soo Line's east–west route across northern Wisconsin (Sault Ste. Marie, Michigan, to Minneapolis via Rhinelander and Ladysmith). Note the handy broom for clearing snow and ice out of switch points in the winter. Trains heading south from here went to Milwaukee and Chicago via Black Creek and Oshkosh. *Bottom photo*: Standing 400 feet from where the track cuts south, with the arrow-straight mainline stretching westward until it vanishes into the distant landscape. In the twenty years since 2002, the tracks going south from Wisconsin Junction have been removed, and service on the east–west route here has been discontinued.

PROGRESS REMAINS: In 2002, the classic "Chesapeake & Ohio For Progress" logo still adorns the side of this drawbridge over the Manistee River in Manistee, Michigan. Over the decades, the line between Manistee and Grand Rapids has been owned by Chesapeake & Ohio and successors Chessie System and CSX. In 2005, Marquette Rail purchased the CSX lines and took over operations on a route that extends from Grand Rapids to Manistee, about 110 miles, with another primary route that cuts west from Walhalla to Ludington, another 16 miles. Marquette Rail, based in Ludington, is a shortline in the Genesee & Wyoming family of railroads.

DOUBLE RED: A freshly painted signal tower protects the drawbridge over the Manistee River at Manistee on Marquette Rail's former CSX trackage.

WHISTLERS: Outside Traverse City in October 2021, a lichen-covered "antique" concrete whistle sign—likely in place here for several decades—is leaning over as if to make way for the modern metal "W" sign installed right behind it. These signs from vastly different eras coexist along this still-active former Chesapeake & Ohio line, which once proceeded north from Traverse City all the way to Bay View, roughly 80 miles up the line. This stretch of track, operated by Great Lakes Central since 2006, now ends in Williamsburg, just 12 miles northeast of Traverse City.

RED DWARF & LOW GREEN: A dwarf signal positioned outside Minnesota Commercial's yard (*left photo*) in St. Paul, Minnesota, protects CP Rail's mainline to Milwaukee where the tracks of the two railroads converge. *Right photo*: At Adams, Wisconsin, a switching move gets a green light from a dwarf signal, allowing a local crew to come off a siding and get back onto the main track on Union Pacific's ex-Chicago & NorthWestern mainline across central Wisconsin.

SCOTTVILLE SUNSET: Late afternoon sunlight reflects off the shiny steel rails in this October 19, 2021, scene captured a few miles west of Scottville, Michigan, on Marquette Rail's ex-C&O line into Ludington.

DIAMOND IN THE ROUGH: A rusting diamond in Tomahawk, Wisconsin, where shortline Marinette, Tomahawk & Western once crossed the mainline of longtime interchange partner Milwaukee Road, has been left to the encroaching weeds. The railroad now connects at Tomahawk with regional carrier Fox Valley & Lake Superior.

TOMAHAWK STOP: Marinette, Tomahawk & Western has undergone significant changes over the years as it has evolved with economic conditions, including reducing its mileage from 14 miles to just 6 miles after key shippers closed their doors. In 2005, the railroad was purchased by Genesee & Wyoming, a corporation that operates numerous railroads across North America. At the time of purchase, the shortline's name was changed to simply Tomahawk Railway.

MIXED HISTORY: A Canadian National freight powered by Wisconsin Central GP40 #3009 and Illinois Central GP40 #3101 rolls slowly eastward on former Green Bay & Western rails near Plover, Wisconsin, on July 12, 2002. WC acquired GB&W in 1993, and CN acquired WC in 2001.

6 MILES OUT OF MUNISING: Wisconsin Central's Munising Local powers south at Munising Junction after handling switching duties in Munising, Michigan, in June 1999. The thrice-weekly local is running on WC's former Lake Superior & Ishpeming branch between Munising Junction and Munising as it starts its return trip to Trout Lake, Michigan, most of which will be on the former Soo Line mainline between Trout Lake and Marquette. This view is from the old Soo Line grade that passes over the ex-LS&I tracks here. In 2022, shortline Grand Elk Railroad took over operating the route from Trout Lake to Munising.

DAWN PATROL: As the first rays of the morning sun begin to filter onto the northern Michigan landscape in the summer of 1999, Wisconsin Central GP35 #2060 is already at work switching the Kimberly-Clark paper mill in Munising.

MILL DUTY: At the same location a dozen summers earlier, in August 1987, Lake Superior & Ishpeming RS3 #1604—built in 1950—is at the Munising mill in the morning, ready to go to work. LS&I sold its isolated 6-mile branch between Munising Junction and Munising to Wisconsin Central in 1990. (*Photo by Dennis Schmidt*)

PULLING TOGETHER: On July 18, 2002, rusting C&NW bay window caboose #10913 rests forgotten on a deadline track in the former C&NW freight yard at Adams, Wisconsin, under a long-obsolete coaling tower. Union Pacific took over the property when it merged C&NW into its rail network in 1995, and with that merger, for the first time, Union Pacific added Wisconsin to the lengthy list of states the celebrated transcontinental carrier serves.

3

Midwest Ghost Dance

LOST SIDING: Summer weeds and rusting steel have taken over this siding at Seney, Michigan, alongside what once was a busy Soo Line main from Sault Ste. Marie to Marquette, Michigan, and on west from there into Wisconsin. The town of Seney was immortalized in "Big Two-Hearted River," a short story by Ernest Hemingway.

FORBIDDEN: Looming out of the morning rain, a weed-overgrown wooden and barbed wire gate blocks off an abandoned Soo Line spur that reached ore loading docks on Lake Superior at Ashland, Wisconsin. These rails were once used to move trainloads of ore to waiting Great Lakes freighters, but the docks were taken out of service in 1965.

GHOST IN THE WOODS: Derelict and forgotten, an abandoned signal tower stands ghostly at Ashland in the northwestern Wisconsin woods on June 23, 1999, as if still protecting Soo Line tracks that once went to an ore loading facility here.

SURVIVORS: The rails of Chicago & NorthWestern once blanketed the state of Wisconsin and Michigan's Upper Peninsula, and the classic C&NW herald was visible in every town with trains passing through. Abandonments in the 1970s/1980s, however, took a heavy toll on the railroad's reach. In 1995, Union Pacific took over C&NW, and more of its remaining routes were sold or abandoned. Yet C&NW still sometimes makes a surprise appearance. This boxcar—C&NW #520055 (*top photo*)—was spotted at Avery, Washington, on July 9, 2022. Although the C&NW succumbed, it outlasted several historic railroads, including Milwaukee Road and Rock Island. After Rock Island fell in 1980, C&NW purchased some of the railroad's assets, such as this boxcar (*bottom photo*) with the Rock's imagery still boldly present in October 1990.

BURIED IN VEGETATION: The Ann Arbor Railroad's main track is still in daily use here, but splintered ties are all that remain of forgotten yard tracks (*left photo*) at railroad-namesake Ann Arbor, Michigan, in June 2006. Until the 1980s, the switching yard here was often congested with freight cars bound for stations to the north and south. In a similar scene a couple hundred miles to the north (*right photo*), ex-Chesapeake & Ohio tracks in the railroad's Boardman Yard in Traverse City, Michigan—now served "as needed" by Great Lakes Central—are overgrown with sumac and other vegetation in October 2021, clearly no longer in use.

RUSTING BRIDGE: The former Chicago & NorthWestern route through Wyeville, Wisconsin, once continued directly southeast on C&NW's own rails to Camp Douglas and Baraboo and then on to reach Madison, Wisconsin's capital city. As of 2023, Union Pacific owns the tracks in Wyeville, but the direct line south through the diamond to Camp Douglas has been removed and this bridge, viewed here on October 18, 2021, has become obsolete infrastructure.

RECONFIGURED: Rusty tracks pointing south come to a sudden halt at Wyeville, just before reaching Union Pacific rails that have skirted the old crossing of two former C&NW routes through this rural community. The new configuration has UP tracks bending in from the east and rejoining the ex-C&NW main to Camp Douglas, 9 miles to the south.

DISAPPEARING ACT: Like the Ann Arbor Railroad itself, which disappeared from this stretch of track soon after the Lake Michigan car ferries stopped operating in April 1982, rails and ties a few miles outside of Elberta, Michigan, vanish into the autumn brush (*top photo*) in this scene from October 1992. Fast forward nearly three decades to the same view (*bottom photo*) from October 2021: The right of way has been transformed into the scenic Betsie Valley Trail, which follows the old railroad route that stretched from Frankfort and Elberta to Thompsonville, roughly 22 miles. The trail opened in 2005.

REBIRTH: Boarded up and abandoned but still standing tall and with its semaphore signals still intact, the former Milwaukee Road depot in Iron Mountain, Michigan—built *circa* 1910—no longer welcomes passengers. The rail line visible on the right in this 2002 photo still hosts freight trains, although Escanaba & Lake Superior, not Milwaukee Road, sets the operating schedules these days. Good news: In recent years, the E&LS has put the old depot back into use as a base for crews handling freight traffic in the area.

NOWHERE ROAD: When Conrail took over Penn Central in 1976, it inherited a fast, CTC-enhanced mainline between Jackson, Michigan, and Elkhart, Indiana, via Three Rivers, Michigan. The route featured remote-controlled sidings that allowed long trains to pass for efficient freight movements. In the early 1980s, priority was given to Conrail's parallel line that cut due west from Jackson to Battle Creek and Kalamazoo before branching south toward Elkhart. As a result, in 1983, the track southwest out of Jackson to Three Rivers was dismantled. This April 2005 scene 6 miles outside Jackson looks west on the once-vital right of way. Compare this dismal view with the 1971 photograph on p. 6 that faces east from this same location.

NOTHING GOING WEST: Once an active east–west mainline across Michigan's Upper Peninsula, the old Soo Line route from Munising Junction to Marquette, Michigan, is in the process of being dismantled in this melancholy scene from the summer of 1999.

PENN CENTRAL POWER: Penn Central locomotives, such as these SD38s waiting for their next assignment in August 1975, were a common sight around the Lower Peninsula of Michigan in the early 1970s. Today, PC's engines, rolling stock, and corporate logo exist only in memories. (*Author's collection*)

ACROSS THE STRAITS: In May 1977, car ferry *Chief Wawatam* is docked in St. Ignace, Michigan, for unloading by a Soo Line crew working out of Trout Lake. *Chief Wawatam*, built in 1911, carried freight cars—and for a time passenger cars—across the Straits of Mackinac, providing a direct rail connection between Michigan's two peninsulas. Soo Line served St. Ignace in the Upper Peninsula, while Pennsylvania Railroad/Penn Central handled Mackinaw City's Lower Peninsula dock. After the 1976 Conrail reorganization, shortlines Michigan Northern and Detroit & Mackinac took over at Mackinaw City, but the ferry operation ended in 1984. (*Photo by Paul Templeton*)

NOT MAKING WAVES: They were once part of a small yet innovative fleet of railroad car ferries moving freight cars back and forth across Lake Michigan. But in September 1997, the railroad car ferry operations are no more, and these three boats—*left to right*, ex-C&O *Spartan*; ex-Ann Arbor *Arthur K. Atkinson*; and ex-C&O *City of Midland 41*—are moored at Ludington, Michigan, retired and destined never again to carry railroad cars or passengers.

GREEN BAY ROUTE NO MORE: Black Creek, Wisconsin: Looking to the west (*top photo*) in 2002 on the right of way of what used to be Green Bay & Western's mainline between Green Bay, Wisconsin, and Winona, Minnesota. Black Creek was once a busy interchange point with Soo Line, but after GB&W was purchased by Wisconsin Central in 1993, much of GB&W's trackage was deemed redundant and abandoned. *Bottom photo:* Boxcars wait on a spur track at Black Creek. The ex-Soo north–south route through Black Creek is now owned by Fox Valley & Lake Superior and operated as far as Shawano, about 25 miles to the north.

HEARTLAND HEARTBREAK: June 22, 2022: An all-too-familiar sight across the United States—tracks paved over and rural railroad crossings dismantled. Only ghosts remain.